Beethoven:
The Man and His Music

written by Robin Doak

illustrated by Marni Backer

McGraw-Hill
School Division

New York   Farmington

Young Beethoven

Have you ever heard of Beethoven (bā´ tō vin)? No, not the dog in the movies! Ludwig van Beethoven, the composer. He was not only a great musician. He wrote his music in spite of a handicap that might have stopped another person.

English Channel

Rhine River

GERMANY

BONN

VIENNA

Paris

AUSTRIA

Madrid

N
W E
S

Rome

Beethoven was born in Bonn, Germany, in 1770. His father and his grandfather were musicians. Little Ludwig loved music. He played piano at four years old! By the age of 12, he was also good at another instrument, the organ. He began to work as an organist's assistant. He also began writing his first music for the piano.

At 17, Ludwig made his first journey to Vienna, Austria. The city was known for its great music.

It was there that Beethoven played the piano for a famous composer. His name was Wolfgang Amadeus Mozart. Mozart had also learned to play when he was very young. He was writing music by the age of five.

Beethoven wanted to stay in Vienna and study with Mozart. But his mother had become ill. His father couldn't care for their two younger sons. So Ludwig went back home. Even after his mother died, Ludwig stayed on in Bonn.

While returning to Vienna from England, another famous composer stopped in Bonn. His name was Franz Josef Haydn. Haydn agreed to accept Ludwig as a student. In 1792, Beethoven returned to Vienna to study with Haydn.

Beethoven loved Vienna. He decided to make his home there. But he needed money. To make some, Ludwig gave his first concert and began teaching piano. He also sold pieces of music that he had written.

In 1800, Beethoven wrote his first symphony. A symphony is a long piece of music that is played by an orchestra. That same year, he also wrote his first ballet. He based it on the story of a giant from the Greek myths.

Soon all of Vienna was talking about Beethoven's music. He was surrounded by the rich and famous people of the city. A few even gave him money each year. They wanted him to stay in Vienna.

Beethoven soon became famous for his musical talent. But he also became famous for his bad manners. He even made fun of the people who gave him money. And he would shout at anyone who didn't like his music.

7

A Silent World

When Beethoven was 30, he began to hear hums and buzzes that no one else could hear. The great composer was going deaf. This would make an enormous change in his life.

Sometimes Beethoven was angry about going deaf. Other times he was sad. At first he tried to keep his problem a secret. Then he made a decision. He would not let being deaf stop him. Beethoven astonished everyone by writing some of his greatest music when he could no longer hear it.

From 1800 to 1808, Beethoven wrote four symphonies. He also wrote many shorter pieces of music. Many people loved his work. It was not like anything that had ever been written before. Beethoven's music was filled with life, joy, and feeling.

Beethoven finally had to use small notebooks to "talk" with his friends. These were called "conversation books." He also used a long horn to hear better. Beethoven would put the horn to his ear and people talked into it.

After a while Beethoven could no longer give piano concerts. He could barely act as conductor for his own music. But that didn't stop him from writing. Beethoven could still "hear" the music in his head.

One of Beethoven's greatest works is his Symphony No. 9. It was his last symphony. It is also known as the "Choral Symphony." It contains a famous part known as the "Ode to Joy."

Beethoven's Symphony No. 9 was first played at a concert in 1824. He had been deaf for about seven years by then. When the concert was over, Beethoven turned around on the stage to face the audience. He was moved to see that they were on their feet and cheering.

Beethoven's last years were quite unhappy. Without many friends or family members to visit him, he was often alone, in a silent world.

In December, 1826, Beethoven became very ill. For four months he was sick. Then, on March 26, 1827, he awoke in bed. As lightning flashed, Beethoven shook his fist at the sky. Then the great composer was gone. He was just 56 years old.

The entire world mourned Beethoven's death. Nearly 20,000 people lined the streets of Vienna to watch his coffin go by.

Beethoven was one of the greatest composers of all time and gave many gifts to the world. He wrote 32 piano sonatas and an opera. He also wrote 9 symphonies, 5 concertos for piano, and a concerto for violin. His music influenced many composers who came after him. The list includes such names as Schubert, Brahms, and Wagner.

Not only is Beethoven's music beautiful, but it has stayed popular all these years. Today, almost two hundred years after his death, millions of people still love his music.